Wonderful Water

Bobbie Kalman & Janine Schaub

Crabtree Publishing Company

Toronto · Oxford · New York

The Primary Ecology Series

To baby Callen

Writing team
Bobbie Kalman
Janine Schaub

Editor-in-chief
Bobbie Kalman

Editors
Janine Schaub
Shelagh Wallace

Design and computer layout
Antoinette "Cookie" DeBiasi

Type output
Lincoln Graphics

Color separations
ISCOA

Printer
Lake Book Manufacturing

Illustrations
Antoinette "Cookie" DeBiasi: cover, title page, pages 7, 16, 26; Lisa Smith: page 10; Barb Bedell: pages 15, 19, 20

Photographs
Rommel/Masterfile: front cover
Antoinette "Cookie" DeBiasi: back cover
Peter Crabtree: pages 4 (top), 8, 12 (bottom right), 27 (bottom), 28, 30 (bottom), 31 (top left), 31 (center right)
Marc Crabtree: title page, pages 4 (bottom), 30 (top)
Jim Bryant: pages 5 (center), 14
Greg Robinson: pages 12 (top), 22, 24-25 (top)
Diane Majumdar: pages 5 (top), 9, 11 (top), 24 (bottom), 25 (bottom)
Courtesy of Health and Welfare: pages 11 (bottom), 31 (top)
Nature Interpretive Center at Royal Botanical Gardens: page 21 (top)
Dave Taylor: page 21 (bottom)
J. Harvey: page 23
Bobbie Kalman: page 6, 12 (bottom left), 13, 27 (top), 29 (both), 31 (bottom)
Courtesy of CIDA/Morrow: page 7
Crabtree Publishing Company made every attempt to secure model releases.

"Jennifer's drop" (pages 16-17) was written by Chris Taylor.

Special thanks to: The students of St. Clare School and Jody Forsyth, their librarian, Jody and Justin Pepe, Victorian Eady (who appears on the back cover), Heather Brissenden, Samantha Crabtree, Bryn Mercer, Andrea Crabtree, Denise Fullerton, Craig Eady, Mark Jones, and Teva Wood

---

Published by
Crabtree Publishing Company

350 Fifth Ave.	360 York Road, R.R.4	73 Lime Walk
Suite 3308	Niagara-on-the-Lake	Headington
New York	Ontario, Canada	Oxford OX3 7AD
N.Y. 10118	L0S 1J0	United Kingdom

Cataloguing in Publication Data
Kalman, Bobbie, 1947-
   Wonderful water

(The Primary ecology series)
Includes index.
ISBN 0-86505-553-X (library bound) ISBN 0-86505-579-3 (pbk.)

1. Water - Juvenile literature.
2. Hydrologic cycle - Juvenile literature.
I. Schaub, Janine. II. Title. III. Series

GB662.3.K35 1992   j551.48

Contents

(above) Many of the first cities were built beside lakes and rivers. When there were no roads, it was easiest to travel by boat. Water was also used for drinking, washing, growing crops, and as power for mills that ground grain, cut wood, and wove cloth. (below) Many people around the world have very little fresh water and must walk a long way to get it.

Keeping our bodies moist

Water is found in tears, mucus, and in our joints. All these fluids help keep our bodies moist and healthy. Water is also needed to wash out the body's waste products, and it plays an important role in controlling body temperature. When you perspire, water comes to the surface of your skin, and your body is cooled down.

Fill 'er up!

Each person's body needs about eight glasses of water each day. Even someone who is resting quietly in the shade loses about four glasses of fluid just by breathing and perspiring. If we lose too much water, we become **dehydrated**. People suffering from dehydration become very thirsty and start to feel tired and very ill. Most people cannot survive more than three days without water.

Water for plants

Like animals and people, every kind of plant needs water to survive. Plants that live in lakes and oceans absorb water from their surroundings. Plants that grow in soil absorb water through their root systems. Water is taken in through the thin hairs that cover the roots. Small tubes in the plant then carry the water and nutrients to the branches and leaves.

Water feels great inside the body and out!

Soaked in color

To see how water travels in a plant, put a few drops of red food coloring in a third of a glass of water. Cut the end off a limp piece of celery and place the stalk in the glass for two or three hours, with the leaves sticking upwards. When you return, you will notice that the tubes within the stalk have pulled the water all the way up into the leaves. Not only is the stalk no longer limp, it also has red color showing where the water has been absorbed.

The three magical forms of water

The next time you make popsicles or ice cubes, you will be taking part in a magical water show.

When you turn on your tap, the water that appears is in its familiar **liquid** form. Pour it into an ice-cube tray or a popsicle mold and place it in the freezer, and water will undergo a magical transformation. It will change into a second form called **ice**!

As you remove your frozen treats from the refrigerator, you may notice a mini-cloud hanging in the air. Although this might seem like an illusion, it is a third form of water called **water vapor**. Water vapor is made up of tiny droplets of water that can float on air. Although water vapor is usually invisible, it becomes visible when warm vapor meets cold air. That is why you can see your breath on a cold day.

Clouds, mist, and fog

When water vapor gets cold, tiny droplets of water form that we can see. These droplets are very light and can float on air. Millions of droplets join together to make clouds.

Sometimes there is a lot of water vapor in the air close to the ground. When this air is suddenly cooled off, the water vapor turns into water droplets that we can see as mist or fog.

Rain

Clouds are made up of millions of droplets of water. Sometimes the droplets join to form big drops. When the drops get too heavy to be held by the clouds, they fall to the earth as rain.

If the sun is shining while it is raining, you will see a **rainbow**. Rainbows are formed when the sun's rays shine through raindrops and break up into bands of color that we see as red, orange, yellow, green, blue, and violet.

Frozen water

When water gets cold, it freezes solid and becomes ice. Ice can be thinner than paper or thicker than a big building. Whatever shape or size ice takes, it can always float in water.

Hail

Sometimes small crystals of ice are blown around inside huge clouds. While they are being tossed up and down, layers of ice form around them. Soon they become solid balls of ice called **hailstones**. When hailstones get too heavy to be held in the clouds, they fall to the ground. The largest hailstone ever found was the size of a melon!

Snow

When the weather is very cold, the water droplets in clouds freeze and form little crystals of ice. The crystals join, and six-sided snowflakes are made. Each snowflake has its own delicate pattern, and each one is different!

Many ways to talk about snow

When we talk about snow, we use words such as wet, dry, and "packing" snow. We do not need many words to describe snow because most of us don't see much of it. The Inuit, on the other hand, live with snow for much of the year. They are aware of all its different forms. For example, they might talk about loose snow, hard snow that has been packed together by the wind, snow that swirls or drifts, snow that forms a bowl around objects, or snow that is like sugar. Can you think of new ways to talk about snow?

The Inuit describe snow and ice in many different ways because they live with both.

Have you ever seen frozen water on a window pane? It looks like beautiful lace.

Two-thirds of the earth is covered in water, but most of that water is too salty to drink. The children in the picture below left are holding a Wholearth Ball, which has been designed to show how Planet Earth looks from space. The large blue areas are the oceans. The children on the right enjoy being in the ocean, but they prefer not to swallow a drop of the salty water. The above picture shows a beautiful sunset over the ocean.

Salt water and fresh water

We live on a planet covered in water, but there is very little fresh water for plants and animals to drink. Almost all the water on earth is salt water found in oceans. Many plants and animals cannot live on salt water. They must, instead, depend on the fresh water that comes from wells, lakes, and rivers.

Salt water

Each day rivers empty their fresh water into the earth's oceans and seas. River water contains small amounts of rock and soil called **mineral salts**. Rivers drain into the oceans, carrying the mineral salts with them. One mineral salt, ordinary table salt, is found in great amounts in the oceans. Table salt gives ocean water a very salty taste.

Tasty water

If you were to taste water from several different areas, you would discover that the water from each region has its own flavor. The taste depends on the **minerals** found in the water. Minerals come from the soil and rocks over which water passes. Water picks up these minerals and, even though we cannot see them, we can taste them!

Have your friends test different kinds of water. Which sample will they like best?

If you were to boil water and collect the drops that formed on the pot lid, you would be left with pure water. Pure water is free of minerals usually found in tap water. Without minerals, pure water has an unpleasant taste.

Water taste test

Most city water has been treated with chemicals that make it clean and safe for drinking. These chemicals flavor the water. Water from wells, lakes, rivers, and springs also have different flavors.

Conduct your own taste test to see which water you prefer. Put bottled water, filtered tap water (tap water drained through a pitcher-type water filter), and ordinary tap water in three different glasses. Take a sip from each and decide which tastes best.

Clean and dirty water

In some areas, water must be collected in large tanks, called **cisterns**, or in huge lakes behind dams, called **reservoirs**. Cisterns and reservoirs store water so there will be plenty even when it does not rain for long periods of time.

Underground water

Rain also soaks into the ground. Using wells, people have learned to bring underground water to the surface. Wells are partly filled with water. The water is pulled up in a bucket on a rope or by using a pump. In some areas, water collects underground and flows to the surface as a freshwater spring.

Millions of people in the world do not have clean water pumped to taps inside their homes, nor is their waste water taken away in sewers and cleaned. Many get sick and die from drinking and washing in unclean water.

Naturally clean water

Water seeps into the ground through many layers of soil, gravel, and rock. During its slow journey, most of the dirt in water is trapped or **filtered** out by the ground materials. When ground water has not been polluted by people, it is naturally clean enough to drink.

Plants are natural water cleaners! They are able to take dirty water into their systems and release clean water into the air, land, and water. Some types of swamp plants clean water so well that they are used to filter water inside **water-treatment facilities**.

Cleaning water for drinking

Once water is found, it is usually piped to a water-treatment facility. Using chemicals, water-treatment facilities clean the water. Filters such as sand and gravel are also used to trap tiny bits of dirt. The water that comes out the other side of these filters is cleaner than it was before.

Indoor plumbing

In homes with indoor plumbing, pumps drain away used water to sewers. Some homes draw fresh water from wells and collect the dirty water in underground septic tanks. These tanks are emptied when they are full.

A water-treatment facility

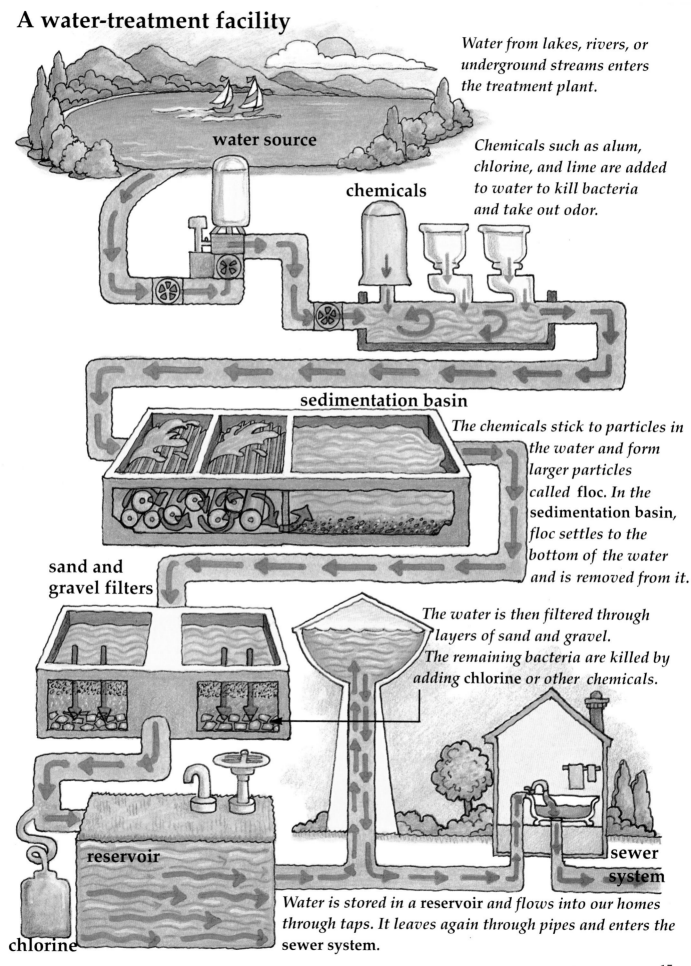

Water from lakes, rivers, or underground streams enters the treatment plant.

water source

chemicals

Chemicals such as alum, chlorine, and lime are added to water to kill bacteria and take out odor.

sedimentation basin

The chemicals stick to particles in the water and form larger particles called floc. In the sedimentation basin, floc settles to the bottom of the water and is removed from it.

sand and gravel filters

The water is then filtered through layers of sand and gravel. The remaining bacteria are killed by adding chlorine or other chemicals.

reservoir

sewer system

chlorine

Water is stored in a reservoir and flows into our homes through taps. It leaves again through pipes and enters the sewer system.

Jennifer's drop

Jennifer's grandfather was a lighthouse keeper on a rocky seashore. Jennifer was very fond of him because he was always kind to her and just a little mysterious.

One summer day, Jennifer and her grandfather sat watching a spectacular show put on by nature. Far below the big lighthouse windows, a storm was playing with the ocean's waves.

"The ocean is so mysterious and magical, Grandpa," she said. The lighthouse keeper smiled, and then a mysterious twinkle came to his eye. "Speaking of magic," he said getting up. "I have a gift for you, Jennie."

The old man shuffled to a corner nook, where he took down an earthen jar which made a sloshing sound.

Jennifer beamed. Her grandfather often entertained her with illusions, like making coins appear from behind her ear. She wondered what magical effect he would produce from the old jar.

"In this jar is a fluid that is millions of years old," Grandfather began. "Each and every drop of this elixir has its own story about the many forms it can take and all the natural things it has been a part of and are a part of it. What would you do if I gave you a drop?"

"I'd drink it right down!" said Jennifer without a moment's hesitation. "Then I could be a part of all those things too!"

"Ah," said Grandfather as he reached into a pocket and produced a long green willow leaf. He dipped the leaf deep into the jar and brought out a single shiny drop that clung to the pointed tip. He held the leaf up to Jennifer so that the light from the window shone through the drop. Jennifer looked into it and, to her amazement, saw the story of the drop's last journey unfolding within.

The story began in a hurricane, far out at sea. Jennifer's drop was carried over a tropical land where it fell on a tender, young plant. It was the time of the dinosaurs, and the drop soon became a part of a great lumbering beast.

For thousands of years, the drop became trapped underground within the bones of the dinosaur until it was dug up and swept away by the wind. Free at last, Jennifer's drop fell again to become part of a seedling, which grew into a giant tree and lived nearly a thousand years. Shed by the grand old tree, the drop next joined a large banana-colored slug and was held inside it by a layer of gooey slime. Caught in the hot sun, the slug could no longer hold the drop and let it go.

From the slimy slug to the sky, the drop rose only to fall yet again, this time into a human-made lake. After a rough trip through a pipe, Jennifer's drop made its way to the kitchen tap of a cabin that was far from the city.

A thirsty boy the same age as Jennifer was the drop's next stop. When the boy skinned his knee on a rocky shore, the drop left him in a tear and fell into the sea where its journey ended.

"Wow," laughed Jennifer, "if that boy ever knew he was connected to a dinosaur or a slug!"

"Or to **you**, Jennie," said her grandfather with a wink. "When you drink that drop, you'll be the first stop on its new journey, which will end—who knows where."

The girl winked back and caught the drop on her tongue. "It's salty!" she said, surprised at the taste.

The mysterious twinkle returned to her grandfather's eye. "Is it?" he said.

Just a few days later, on her first day of school, Jennifer sat beside a boy who smiled at her. Somehow, Jennifer was not surprised to see that the boy had a large scrape on one knee. She smiled warmly back.

The water cycle

As you have read in the story "Jennifer's drop," the water that we see on our earth has been here since the planet was formed. In all that time, no more water has been added to the earth's supply. Water is forever traveling into the air and back onto the earth again. This constant circling is called the **water cycle**.

Evaporation and condensation

The sun heats the water found in lakes, rivers, and oceans. Its heat lifts and carries tiny water drops in the air. This is called **evaporation**. When the water drops cool down, they form clouds. The water in clouds then **condenses**, or turns to liquid, and falls from the sky as **precipitation**. Precipitation can be snow, sleet, hail, or rain.

Back to the ocean

Precipitation can end up in many places. Some falls back into the sea, and some drops onto the land. In the end, however, all water returns to the ocean. This happens because water always flows from higher to lower ground, and **sea level** is the lowest level of ground.

Water does not go directly to the ocean. It can soak into the soil, stay underground, or be absorbed by the roots of plants. Water may stay trapped in these areas for thousands of years! At some point, though, water will end up in a river and begin its final journey to the ocean. It may stay in the ocean for years or evaporate the next day to begin the cycle of evaporation, condensation, and precipitation all over again.

Transpiration and perspiration

Some of the water that falls to earth is used by plants and animals. As plants and animals use water, they also give off water into the air around them.

Plants release water into the air through their leaves. This process is called **transpiration**. Some animals release water by panting, whereas other animals and people, release it through **perspiration**, or sweating.

Water never leaves the earth

All the water that you see around you has been up in the air and has fallen back to the earth many, many times. Water is constantly evaporating and condensing. Its cycle never ends! Although water may collect in puddles, pass through living creatures, form clouds, and fall all over the world, it never leaves our planet.

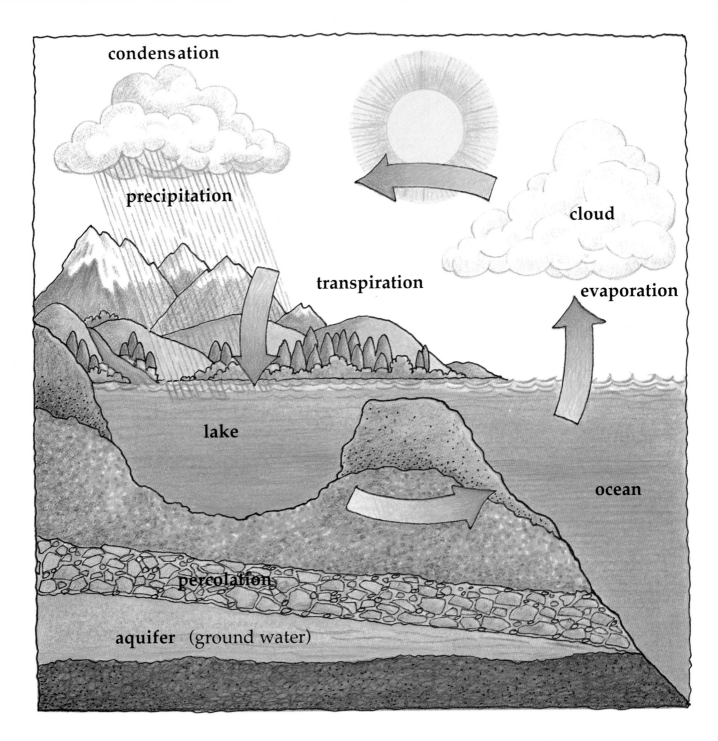

condensation

precipitation

transpiration

cloud

evaporation

lake

ocean

percolation

aquifer (ground water)

The journey of water

When a lot of rain or snow falls, not all the water is absorbed by the soil. Some of the precipitation creates **runoff**. Runoff is water that "runs off" the surface of the ground and fills rivers and lakes. The water found in rivers and lakes is called **surface water** because it is above the ground. Some precipitation moves down, or **percolates**, through holes in the soil and ends up as **ground water**. Ground water supplies millions of people around the world with drinking water. It is brought to the surface using wells or pumps. Rocks, clay, sand, and gravel store large underground sources of water called **aquifers**.

Pond habitats

Loons dive for fish, bats skim the surface for insects, and blue herons stalk the shorelines for frogs—the pond is a home for thousands of plants and animals. Racing whirligig beetles and water scorpions dodge duckweed on the pond surface. Mosquito larvae and water scavenger beetles move just below the surface of the water.

Cattails, rushes, and grasses near the pond's edge provide shelter for many birds, frogs, worms, and insects. Small fish may take cover under the water lilies that float in the shallow water. Farther into the open pond, fish, turtles, and water birds swim around plants and tiny animals that drift in the deeper water.

A trip to a pond

With a friend and an adult, plan a trip to a nearby pond or stream. Be sure to wear comfortable clothes and rubber boots. Bring along a pail, a glass jar, and a pad and pencil.

Sensing nature

When you get to the pond, move quietly to the water's edge. Spend a few minutes just looking and listening. Do you see any animals that are making the pond their home? Where are all the noises you hear coming from? What smells do you detect?

Sketch five different plants that grow beside the water. Sketch five more that grow right at the shoreline and five that grow in the water. Can you name any of the plants? If you were a frog-sized pond animal, where would be the best spot for you to stay out of sight?

Crowded waters

Carefully scoop up a jar full of pond water. Set it down on the shore and allow it to settle. After a few moments, look at the different kinds of plants and creatures that are floating or swimming around in the water.

Take a bit of water back to your school. With the help of a teacher, look at a drop of pond water under a microscope. The magnifying lens will allow you to see the creatures in the water that are too small to be seen with your naked eye.

You will be surprised by all the life in the pond. Your samples may include weeds, crayfish, insects, and other tiny water creatures.

Use a jar and net to catch and store samples. To prevent "soakers," pick up a dead branch and poke the bottom of the pond to see how deep it is in front of you.

Water that cuts and carves

Long ago, our planet looked very different than it does today. Flowing and falling water and crashing waves have caused many of the changes that have taken place on the earth's surface. Water can break apart rocks and wear them down into sand. It can carry away loose stones and soil and drop them in other places. Over time, water can move mountains, carve valleys, and completely change the way a whole area appears.

Rivers of ice

At many times during our planet's history, the weather was cold for long periods. During those periods, snow fell and stayed. The snow built up over thousands of years and was sandwiched to form thick layers of ice called **glaciers**. Glaciers are frozen rivers that move slowly over the earth.

The ice in glaciers is very hard and heavy. It is able to cut and shape the land over which it passes. Glaciers can slice off the tops of mountains or carve out valleys. Glaciers can polish and grind rock and move these materials thousands of kilometers!

A glacier looks like a dirty frozen river.

Mini-river experiment

The next time you are playing in the sand, bring a pail of water with you and try the following "mini-river" experiment.

Make a trough in the sand that is higher at one end than the other. Find some small stones of various sizes and put them at the high end of the trough. Slowly dump your pail of water over the stones. After the water has run its course, take a look at the positions of the little stones. Which stones were moved the farthest? What happened to the sand at the bottom and sides of the trough? How does your "mini-river" experiment show some of the work water carries out in real rivers?

Spectacular waters

Most people love water and will travel great distances to be close to it. They visit lakes, rivers, and oceans to enjoy activities such as sailing, swimming, fishing, or surfing. Some forms of water are so different and exciting that people are thrilled just to see them.

Waterfalls such as Niagara Falls, shown below, attract millions of visitors. Hot springs are also fascinating, especially when they have formed huge limestone terraces such as the ones found at Mammoth Hot Springs in Yellowstone National Park. The terraces look like ice with hot water bubbling over them. Underground rivers (opposite bottom) form as water trickles down through tiny holes in rocks. Eventually, huge caverns are carved out by the water.

Water activities

People of all ages love to play in and around water. With your friends, try some of the water games and activities on these two pages.

Water music

Collect eight narrow-necked glass bottles of the same size. Pour a different amount of water into each one. Tap the bottles gently with a stick or pencil. You will notice that the more water there is, the higher the sound you make will be. Arrange the bottles from lowest to highest sound, making a musical scale. Now play a tune.

You may produce similar results by blowing over the rims of the bottles. Place your bottom lip on the rim of one of the bottles. Blow hard enough to make a sound. This activity requires a lot of deep breathing. If you feel the least bit dizzy, do not continue.

An eggsperiment

You need the following supplies:
- one glass of water
- one glass of salt water (mix 10 mL/2 teaspoons of salt with 500 mL/2 cups of water)
- two eggs

Put one egg in the fresh water and observe the results. Put the other egg in the salt water. What happens?

Water poster

Water is precious to each one of us. Get your friends and classmates to design posters that illustrate how water is important to them. Decorate your classroom with your artwork.

Underwater conversation

The next time you are swimming with a friend, try having a conversation underwater. How does the water change the sound of your voices? Is it easier or more difficult to hear noises underwater? Move farther apart and try talking to each other. How well do your voices carry over the distance?

Water-relay race

Each year most schools have a game day at which relay races are played. One game that stresses water conservation is played by having the members from two teams fill containers with teaspoons of water.

One at a time, each person carries his or her teaspoon several meters to the team's cup without spilling any of the water along the way. The team that conserves the most water during its trips and fills its container first is the winner.

The blue heron's secret

Blue herons are experts at catching frogs as they swim underwater. This feat is more difficult than it looks because water bends light as the light passes through it. This means that when you spot a frog underwater, it is really in a slightly different location than where you are seeing it.

Blue herons know exactly how much the water is bending the light and make up for this difference each time they strike. The next time you are diving for objects in a swimming pool, try to discover the blue heron's secret.

Heather is running carefully so that she will not waste water. Are you using water carefully each and every day?

Will you discover the blue heron's secret?

Water pollution

The supply of water on our earth always remains the same. The water that we drink today has been used over and over again since before the dinosaurs lived on our planet. The water supply that we are using now will be used by people, plants, and animals in the future. Water pollution is dangerous to creatures that are living now and to the ones that will be born in the years ahead.

The chart below shows types of pollution that threaten water supplies all over the world:

Water does not mix with oil. Oil that spills into water ends up coating the surface, sinking in globs to the bottom, or washing up on beaches, as shown above.

Acid rain
Dangerous gases from factories and cars mix with water vapor in the air. When this water vapor turns to rain, it can be as acidic as vinegar! Over time, acid rain can kill trees, fish, and lakes.

Pollution from farming
Chemicals used by farmers to kill bugs and weeds are poisonous to people and animals and unsafe for drinking or washing. Animal waste and leftover milk also cause pollution when they are flushed into local sewers.

Thermal pollution
Water is used in factories to cool down such materials as red-hot steel. When hot waste water is dumped into lakes and rivers, the result is **thermal pollution**. Thermal pollution causes many plants and animals to die.

Sewage
Large amounts of human waste, called **sewage**, can pollute water by making it unsafe for drinking, washing, or swimming.

Industrial pollution
Liquid wastes from many different kinds of factories are dumped into our water systems. These wastes contain dangerous chemicals that can kill plants and animals.

Oil pollution
Whenever oil is transported by ship across water, there is a danger that it will spill. Oil kills many kinds of plants and animals in the water and on the shores. Sea otters lick it off their fur and die. Water birds become covered in oil and are unable to fly or swim. Their oil-coated feathers no longer protect them from cold weather, and they die.

Conserving our water supplies

When we turn on our taps, fresh water comes pouring out. We are so used to having plenty of water that we hardly ever think about saving it. In many parts of the world, people have very little fresh water, and the water that is available to them is polluted.

A limited supply

Although two-thirds of the earth is covered in water, there is very little fresh water on which all people, plants, and animals depend. We all take our water from this limited supply, and we use it over and over again. It is important not to waste water and to keep it clean for living creatures all over the world. Not wasting water and keeping it clean is called **water conservation**.

Conserving water at home

Here are some simple ways you can conserve water in your home:
• Place a plastic bottle full of water in the toilet tank away from the flushing mechanism. The bottle will take up some of the space normally filled by water. With each flush, your family will use less water.
• Wash your hands with cold water. You waste water as you let the tap run while you are waiting for the warm water to arrive.

• Don't run water while you brush your teeth. You can save a lot of water by turning off the tap.
• Make sure your family washes only full loads of laundry.
• Have short showers instead of baths.
• If you do have a bath, use the water to wash a floor or your dog.
• Collect rain water in a tub or barrel and use it for watering plants and for washing the family car.

Wonderful water!

Splash, jump, squirt, and make waves in it—water can be such fun. The children pictured on these two pages are enjoying many water activities. Have you ever wrestled an alligator, shot down white-water rapids in a giant tire, searched for shells by the seashore, taken an icy dip in an arctic pond, or kicked up your heels in the ocean surf? What are your favorite water activities?

Glossary

acid rain Rain that has become polluted by gases from factories and cars

aquifer A large source of underground water stored in rock, clay, or sand

cell The basic unit of all living things

cistern A natural or human-made tank that stores liquid, especially rain water

condensation The changing of gas to a liquid

conservation Protection from loss, harm, or waste, especially of natural resources

dehydrate To lose water or moisture

elixir A cure for every ailment

evaporation The changing of a liquid to a gas or vapor

glacier A large piece of ice that moves slowly over the earth's surface

ground water Water that is beneath the surface of the earth

mineral Any substance that occurs in nature and is neither animal nor vegetable

mucus A thick, slimy fluid

nutrient Anything that nourishes

percolate To drip through small spaces or holes

perspiration The moisture given off through the pores of the skin

pollution The state of being impure or dirty

precipitation Any form of water that falls to the earth

reservoir A natural or human-made lake that stores water

runoff Surface streams caused by rain or snow that are not absorbed by the soil

sewage Waste disposed of through sewers

surface water The water in rivers and lakes

transpiration The giving off of waste that is in the form of a gas by a living thing

vapor Invisible water that is present in the air

water cycle The constant cycle of evaporation, condensation, and precipitation

Index

2 3 4 5 6 7 8 9 0 Printed in USA 1 0 9 8 7 6 5 4 3